ILLUSTRATED
WOODTURNING
TECHNIQUES

ILLUSTRATED WOODTURNING TECHNIQUES

JOHN HUNNEX

GUILD OF MASTER CRAFTSMAN PUBLICATIONS LTD

First published 1996 by Guild of Master Craftsman Publications Ltd
166 High Street · Lewes · East Sussex · BN7 1XU

Designed by Martin Lovelock

Set in Monotype Dante

Origination supervised by MRM Graphics

Printed in Hong Kong by H&Y Printing Ltd

CONTENTS

Acknowledgements   vi

Introduction   1

1 Approaches   3

2 Bowls   9

3 Closed forms   31

4 Natural tops   49

5 Vases   65

6 Hollow forms   83

7 Bottles   101

Bibliography   120

Index   121

ACKNOWLEDGEMENTS

My thanks go to:

David Ellsworth for the inspiration he has provided for me over the years, and for the way he has helped to raise the profile of woodturning internationally.

Rye Art Gallery, Rye, East Sussex, for their encouragement and support over the years.

Kent Arts and Libraries for giving me the opportunity to exhibit my work to a wider public.

John Harrison of Selwood Saw Mills, Faversham, Kent, for giving me the opportunity to acquire unusual and interesting timbers in the sizes I require.

Axminster Power Tool Centre, Axminster, Devon, for making various accessories for my 4-jaw chucks.

Jonathan Ingoldby, my editor at GMC Publications, and Ian Penberthy, for helping me with the text of this book.

INTRODUCTION

This book naturally follows on from *Woodturning: A Source Book of Shapes*, and is the result of numerous requests from people wanting to know more about the tools and techniques I use to produce some of the forms illustrated in the first book (such as bowls, natural top pieces and hollow forms), and about the way in which my own background in the craft has shaped my ideas and approaches.

I have assumed the reader has already acquired the essential turning skills and techniques, so consequently I do not devote time to topics such as general use of lathes, or the difference between hardwoods and softwoods. However, I do devote time to those elements of the turning process which directly affect the design and turning of my own functional and ornamental pieces, and through this hope to demonstrate that such 'advanced' work is within the grasp of all competent turners, providing they take the right approach.

Like *A Source Book of Shapes*, this book relies heavily on illustration to convey the tremendous possibilities which turning offers for creativity and variety of form. It is essential that you be able to see the designs and, I hope, be inspired to experiment with form yourself.

This introduction and the chapter on approaches are followed by six illustrated chapters, each devoted to a different type of turned form. The first part of each chapter demonstrates the tools and techniques required to produce that form, and the second part consists of a gallery of pieces produced in this way, showing the tremendous variation which can be achieved within each style.

It is worth noting that all the photographs in the techniques sections were taken working on the inboard side of the lathe. If you prefer to work on the outboard side, you would of course take up the opposite position because of the opposite rotation.

I hope very much that you will find useful, practical information and some inspiration for your own turning in the pages that follow.

An example of a hollow form (see Chapter 6), turned from burr elm. This particular piece was 7in (178mm) high and 9in (229mm) wide, and was finished with two coats of Danish oil.

CHAPTER ONE

APPROACHES

BACKGROUND

I first encountered woodturning in 1943, when our woodwork teacher demonstrated the technique on a lathe at school, using a piece of wood salvaged from a bomb-site (there was hardly any wood available commercially for teaching purposes during the war). He turned a column, and then showed us how to turn beads and coves. He allowed me to attempt turning myself (very unsuccessfully), but the experience awakened my interest in the craft, and I determined one day to master it.

Fourteen years later, in 1957, I bought my first lathe, a Coronet Minorette combination machine, as I also needed a flatbed electric saw at that time. I was given a demonstration of how to turn an egg-cup and a bowl before taking the lathe home, and from that moment was well and truly hooked. Later I supplemented this machine with a Myford ML8 with a ¾ HP motor, which served me very well for many years. Eventually I exchanged this for a Harrison Graduate short bed lathe, and had a 1½ HP motor and a foot stop switch fitted. By removing the rear rest and adding a tripod T-rest, I am able to produce the larger work which I enjoy. This

lathe also allows me to turn up to 15¾in (400cm) between centres. I have also acquired a Robert Sorby lathe – the RS2 model – with a bowl-turning attachment and stand. Both lathe and stand are easily dismantled, an added bonus in that it allows me to transport my own equipment to demonstrations, avoiding the problems inherent in trying to demonstrate on an unfamiliar lathe. Everything I need fits comfortably into my small hatchback car!

In my early days as a turner I quickly tired of turning salt and pepper pots and simple bowls, and began to look for other types of turning. I was initially inspired by some of the pieces in Ernst Rottger's *Creative Wood Craft* (1961), and as a result turned some very thin-walled bowls and began to use carving tools for the first time, to create scalloped tops on some pieces. These received a rather mixed reception, and I began to become discouraged until I came across Gerald T. James's book *Woodturning Design and Practice* (1958, now unfortunately out of print), which contained examples of the work of Finn Juhl from Copenhagen. I had not seen non-cylindrical turning before, and I realized for the first time the importance of shape over technique. This encouraged me to continue my experiments with shape and form, and ignore the negative reactions I was receiving to some of my work.

In 1950 I had managed to secure a two-year traineeship in press photography with the *Kentish Mercury* (now the *Kentish Times*). I was delighted, as ever since childhood I had hoped one day to be some form of commercial artist, and the apprenticeship served as my gateway to a career in photography. By 1967 I was a lecturer in photography at Goldsmiths College, and this along with other photographic assignments meant that woodturning had to take second place for some 15 years! I did manage to keep my hand in, however, and found the craft to be a great therapy. My time at Goldsmiths brought me into contact with students of fine art, sculpture, ceramics, textiles and many other crafts. Their imaginative and challenging approach to traditional techniques once again brought home to me the fact that the conventional way is not necessarily the only way.

I was forced to retire in 1984 due to ill health, and as a result I had time to begin turning in earnest again, impressed and inspired by the revolutionary work of such turners as David Ellsworth and his hollow forms, and Lech Zielinski, whose articles first introduced me to green turning, as well as Bert Marsh, Mark Lindquist and Jim Partridge.

I was fired up with all my old enthusiasm, and when in 1987 I saw an advertisement for an international woodturning seminar to be held in Loughborough, I responded immediately. It was at that meeting that the Association of Woodturners of Great Britain was formed, with myself as one of the founder members.

In the same year I was offered a one-man show of my work at the Ashford Gallery in Kent, organized by Kent Arts and Libraries. There I met the proprietor of The Turning Point woodturning centre at Biddenden, and he invited me to demonstrate to local turners. This was a wonderful opportunity for me in many ways, not least in that it helped to reduce the necessary self-enforced isolation that the craft requires.

It was also around this time that I first met an American turner, Dave Crawford, who invited me to join the American Association of Woodturners, and I went with him to my first American woodturning seminar in Seattle. Going to the USA completely revolutionized my thinking in terms of the combination of turning, carving and innovative sculptural woodturning. I found the Americans to be extremely open to new ideas, and receptive to innovative work, which attitude in turn fosters the growth and development of such work. I found the whole experience extremely refreshing, and encountered many talented woodturners producing exciting and highly creative work.

Since my return, my aim has always been to try to be constantly innovative, and I hope very much that this book will help and inspire you to do the same.

DESIGN

Some turners regard technique as more important than design. While technique is necessary, I believe that, once it has been mastered, then design should become a primary consideration.

A design can be functional or ornamental. If you're making a functional bowl – to hold fruit, for example – your design will be influenced by the need for an open top and an adequate base, so that the bowl does not topple over when filled. A non-functional piece, on the other hand, allows you to have, for example, a closed top and a narrow base. Such a piece is ornamental, and its 'shape' and 'form' are not compromised by the constraints of function. Such pieces in effect allow you total freedom of expression.

There are two basic design principles which affect the type of shapes produced by woodturning: curves and proportion. Train your eye to look for the continuous flowing movement of a curve, and the relationship between one part of the work and another, crucial to the achievement of good proportions. A study of oriental ceramics, which have produced some exceptionally beautiful curved forms, will teach you a great deal.

Design sense can improve through the experience of working in a particular medium over a period of time. For turners, wood offers enormous variety and endless possibilities. The more you turn, the better you get to know your materials and the more accomplished you become, both technically and in terms of the shapes you produce.

Wood that has been turned to a beautiful shape is a lovely thing to handle. People like smooth, round objects (when have you not been tempted to pick up a pebble on a beach?), but the shape has to be right to make you want to pick it up in the first place.

Three practical points: first, I think it is important to have a clear idea of the shape you wish to achieve before you begin, and to make a rough drawing of it for reference as you proceed. Try not to be distracted in any way from being clearly focused on your intended shape and design. I do not generally subscribe to the view that good results can be achieved by putting a piece of wood on the lathe, beginning to turn and seeing what happens. Although I appreciate that this approach has a dedicated following, I feel that it leaves too much to chance.

Second, try not to allow your chuck to control or influence the proportion of your designs; the base of a piece should be in proportion to the body of the work, and the chucking method should be chosen with this in mind.

Third, when you stop the lathe during turning, do not let the pretty wood 'talk to you' by persuading you it is too beautiful for any more to be cut away. This will only cause you to deviate from your original design conception. There are exceptions of course; occasionally, when you are shaping the wood, you may come across hidden fissures, cracks or splits and unless you can successfully incorporate these into your design to enhance its effect, you may have to find another blank and begin again.

It is important that you learn to be critical of your own work, while at the same time striking a balance between complimentary and not-so-complimentary comments from others. In this way you will be able to progress, and develop an appreciation of the fact that form is equally, if not more, important than the wood or the technique used to create it.

HEALTH AND SAFETY

Different people react differently to different woods, and there is a myriad of widely differing allergies to woods and especially to wood saps. It is essential to be aware of this, and to guard against it.

The answer is to play safe at all times. Protect yourself against sap by wearing gloves. Rubber gloves are one option, but thick gardening gloves are also good protection and I favour them over rubber, finding it easier to work with them on. Protect yourself against dust by wearing a respirator helmet (right). I also highly recommend a work-jacket which zips right up to the neck; these are specially made for woodturners, and are available from any woodturning equipment supplier.

*The shallow bowl turned for this chapter was made from figured
beech, and measured 2 x 10in (51 x 254mm) as a finished piece.*

CHAPTER TWO

BOWLS

Wooden bowls have been made for centuries, first by hand carving, later turned on lathes. The first turned bowls were probably made by the Etruscans around 400BC, on primitive lathes also constructed from wood, and the earliest pictorial record we have dates from Egypt around 300BC. While bowls are one of the first functional items made by turners, and are still thought of by many as primarily functional items, they are now also being accepted as decorative items in their own right.

My preference for bowl (faceplate) turning in general came to me quite early on in my woodturning life. I came to the decision that most spindle turning consists of repetition work – four matching chair legs for example, or numerous matching banister spindles, and this held little appeal for me. The only

repetiton work I do in bowl turning is an aspect of preparation necessitated by the nature of wet wood and the rarity of available dry wood. Wet wood shrinks and distorts as it dries, and it takes many years for any piece of wood thicker than 6in (152mm) to dry thoroughly. To shorten this drying time, I 'rough turn' blanks to the shapes I require, to a thickness of 1in (25mm), and leave these to dry for 6 to 12 months. I then return them to the lathe to be 'trued up' and finished.

Bowls take on their own individuality through their shape and form. Apart from treen, it is quite rare that one is asked to make matching bowls. Their appeal for me therefore lies in the myriad of different sizes and shapes that can be produced. The shape and curve of a simple bowl is a challenge which is often overlooked.

TURNING A FIGURED BEECH BOWL

I use a centre finder to locate the faceplate on the blank, which requires the centre of the blank to be marked with a small punch or bradawl.

Push the pin of the centre finder dowel into the wood. Place the faceplate over the dowel, and screw it to the blank (four screws are sufficient for a small bowl) so that the screws penetrate to about ½in (13mm). You can see I have made a permanent reference mark on the edge of this faceplate. When the faceplate is fixed a matching reference mark is made on the wood, providing a ready location point should you need to remount the faceplate at any time.

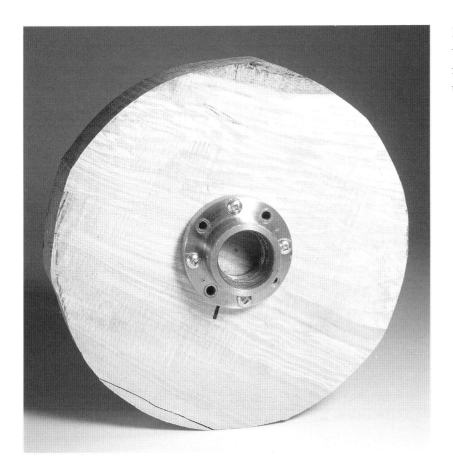

Remove the dowel; the
work is ready to be
mounted on the lathe for
turning.

The tapered Mick O'Donnell jaws used in this
chapter will allow sanding almost to the
bottom of the bowl.

11

For this bowl I chose to turn a dovetailed spigot for the contracting jaws, while rough turning the external shape of the bowl at the same time. This enabled me to utilize as much of the depth of the wood as possible.

Once the shape had been rough turned, I mounted the bowl on to the chuck and turned the underside ready for sanding. Before commencing sanding, I sheer cut the shape for a fine finish. Another way is to finish the outside shape before reversing.

When starting on the inside, I first made a V-mark to show the width I required for the rim. Then, using a ⅜in (10mm) diameter bit, I drilled a guide hole to indicate the maximum depth to which I could cut; once the bottom of the hole was reached, I knew I should cut no further. When drilling this hole it is important to stop short of the intended bottom of the bowl by about ⅛in (3mm), which allows for finishing cuts and sanding.

Here I have begun the cut. Note the position of the gouge at this stage; as you push forward, roll the tool to the left ...

... until you reach the centre.

Work your way across the facia of the bowl,
cut by cut ...

... until you reach the rim mark. Do not cut deeper than half-way down into the bowl. Leaving some bulk in the bowl while you cut the rim will help support it as it becomes thinner.

When starting to undercut the rim, push firmly with your thumb to avoid 'kickback'.

Cut the outer rim to shape using a ¼in (6mm) gouge.

You will find the ¼in (6mm) gouge very useful for fine undercutting, but the tool limits the amount by which you can cut under the rim.

I used a ⅜in (10mm) cranked scraper to finish undercutting the rim. It is a good finishing tool that gives a very smooth surface.

The tip of the cranked scraper. This type of scraper is available in a variety of sizes; the HSS tip can be ground to suit your needs, and can easily be rotated for left-handed use. It can also be rotated at an angle of 40–60 degrees, allowing it to double as a sheer scraper.

Make regular checks of the thickness of the bowl's 'wall' using calipers. You can see that I use plastic ear plugs on the ends of my calipers. These prevent the tool from scratching the work after sanding and polishing, but do not make it any less accurate.

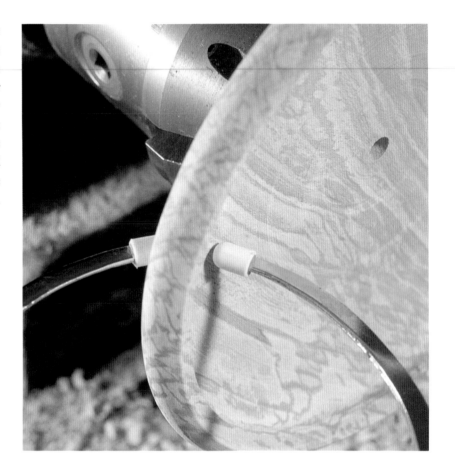

With the rim finished I went back to hollowing the bowl, making light cuts towards the centre using a ¼in (6mm) bowl gouge. I used a small gouge here to aid depth control, as at this stage the bowl is quite thin.

As the wall of the bowl approaches the finished thickness, make light cuts towards the centre, avoiding excessive pressure – this is now becoming a delicate piece! This process will make for a smooth, even finish.

Any remaining ridges on the bowl should be removed; I used a heavy-duty ¼in (6mm) thick round-nosed scraper to sheer cut these away.

The work is now ready for sanding and finishing.

I used wooden jaws mounted on a 4-jaw chuck to hold the bowl by the rim, allowing me to shape the 'foot' of the bowl.

The wooden jaws were held to the chuck by means of wood jaw plates (left). These accessories allow you to make your own wood jaws of a size to match the workpiece, which is offered up to the dovetail rim of the wooden jaws, and the jaws expanded until the work is held firmly.

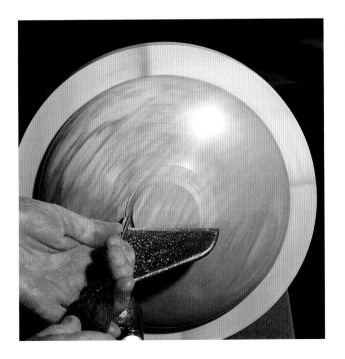

I used a miniature gouge to cut the foot to its final shape as this tool ensures that light cuts are taken.

The base of the finished piece; as with all my pieces, I turned the bottom of the foot slightly concave to ensure that the bowl would stand flat.

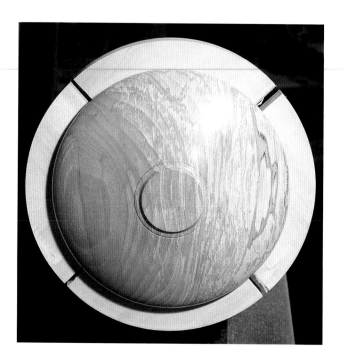

The finished piece.

GALLERY

Wood: Red river gum · Height: 5in (127mm) · Width: 12½in (318mm)
Finish: Three coats of Danish oil

This attractive Australian timber has a very strong colour with darker mottled undertones. Here, the inner curve does not follow the outer as one might expect. Other design features are the definite rim on the outer wall made with a small bead, and the small, delicate rim on the top.

Wood: Rainbow wood (dyed and laminated plywood)
Height at highest point: 2¾in (70mm) · Width: 6¼in (158mm)
Finish: Melamine and clear paste wax

*This piece was turned 'off centre', with the underside turned
to a V shape, allowing the bowl to find its own level when placed
on a shelf.*

Wood: Cedar · Height: 3in (76mm) · Width: 13in (330mm)
Finish: Two coats of paste wax

Cedar reacts well to sandblasting, producing a beautiful textured effect, and this was my original plan for this simple bowl. However, I changed my mind when I saw the strong and attractive grain pattern emerging as the bowl was turned; a rare example of my letting the 'pretty wood' talk to me, at least in terms of the finishing if not the design of the piece itself!

Wood: Spalted beech · Height: 4in (102mm)
Width: 16in (406mm) · Finish: Four coats of Danish oil

I used sisal rope as a feature on this bowl, threaded through four lugs
formed by turning a rim on the outside of the bowl and then cutting away
the areas not required with a bandsaw. Holes were then carefully drilled
through the lugs, beginning with a small drill and gradually increasing the
drill-bit size until the correct width of hole was achieved. As the colour of
the rope blended well with the wood I left it in its natural state.

Wood: Sonokeling · Height: 4in (102mm) · Width: 9in (229mm)
Finish: Two coats of Danish oil

This piece could almost be said to be a closed form
(see Chapter 3) but was turned with the aim of producing
a deep bowl with a strong rim.

Wood: Wenge · Height: 2¼in (57mm)
Width: 11in (279mm) · Finish: Three coats of Danish oil

*With this bowl the light ring cut into the top edge was
sufficient decoration, emphasizing the simplicity of the piece.*

Wood: Boxwood · Height: 3in (76mm)
Width: 8in (203mm) · Finish: Melamine and paste wax

I often try to emulate the simplicity of oriental pottery in my work, and its influence can easily be seen in this piece. The bowl has been turned fairly thin to give the impression of delicacy, which is further enhanced by the subtle curve of the lip. This particular piece of boxwood had attractive and unusual markings in the grain which appealed to me very much.

The closed form turned for this chapter was made from figured ash, and measured 7 x 13in (178 x 330mm) as a finished piece.

CHAPTER THREE

CLOSED FORMS

Turned closed forms are similar to containers made in many parts of the world to hold dry goods. The opening at the top is just wide enough for a hand to reach in and collect a handful of the contents but is easily covered to prevent invasion by insects. Therefore, these forms can be termed 'functional', but they can also have great beauty, retaining the grain pattern that normally would be lost in the turning of a standard bowl form.

A closed form can either have a rim turned from the same blank, or a contrasting rim cut from another species of wood to add emphasis and interest. Unlike a hollow form, in which the opening is too small to gain any useful access to the interior, a closed form can be hand finished on the inside. The term 'closed' refers to the manner in which the sides of the piece 'close over' the top. This type of vessel has an air of mystery about it, which I find very appealing.

TURNING A CLOSED FORM

The rough turned closed form mounted on the lathe ready for final shaping. I used a hook tool from the Stewart system (See pages 71 and 88) to true up the inside of the vessel, ready for sanding later on.

Cleaning up the opening. You can see how much the vessel has distorted around the rim during the drying process. As a result, it is very important to ensure the cut is square.

I began reshaping the exterior of the closed form with a ⅜in (10mm) gouge using a pushing cut. This size of gouge is ideal for both roughing and fine cutting.

Here the same gouge is used with a pulling motion, producing a less clean cut, but one which removes the wood more quickly.

A sheer cut using a 1½ (38mm) skew scraper ground to a shallow bevel finishes the exterior shape. Pull the tool across the face of the work at an angle of around 45 to 60 degrees. If you cut with the bottom two thirds of the blade, it will not dig in in the way conventional scrapers can when used flat on the tool rest.

The inner wall of the opening must be square; if not, it must be cleaned up. The bowl is now ready for sanding to a fine finish. The shavings you can see are those from the sheer cutting tool.

Instead of cutting a raised rim on this vessel, I opted for a contrasting rim. This required a collar joint to be turned, a flat 'shoulder' being cut around the opening as shown.

It is vital that the shoulder around the rim of the vessel is flat to allow maximum adhesion between the adhesive and the wood. After turning the collar joint, check this using a rule held on edge.

The disc of wood for the rim should be cut ⅝in (16mm) wider than the opening in the vessel. Drill a ¼in (6mm) diameter hole through the centre and then mount the disc on a screw chuck. Measure the opening in the bowl with calipers, and draw a corresponding circle, a fraction wider, on the disc. Keep the calipers set at this width; you will need them later. Use a parting tool to cut a ¼in (6mm) wide shoulder down to the pencil mark. To demonstrate the techniques clearly, a deliberately contrasting wood blank has been shown rather than the actual blank used for the rim.

The face of the shoulder must be flat, so stop the lathe and check this with a rule.

Offer up the body of the vessel to the shoulder of the disc. If it is does not fit, remove a fraction of wood at a time from the shoulder until you achieve a snug fit. When you are happy, apply adhesive to the mating faces and glue the rim into the main body.

The hole in the disc allows air to escape from the vessel as it is pushed home, ensuring good contact between the adhesive, rim and main body. Allow the adhesive to harden. Mount the closed form back on the lathe and use the calipers to mark the size and position of the opening on the face of the disc. Cut a groove inside this mark with a small parting tool, and then cut through the disc completely. (You can save the resulting smaller disc for another similar job.)

Here the correct rim piece is shown in place,
ready for final shaping.

Once the rim has been cut
to shape, the inside and
outside of the vessel can be
sanded ready for three
coats of Danish oil,
allowing 24 hours between
each coat.

Here the closed form has been reversed and mounted on an expanding 4-jaw chuck with wood plates that grip the inside of the rim, ready for shaping and trimming the base. The tailstock is used to secure the bowl for safety; for the same reason, a slower cutting speed is required in this mode to minimize vibration.

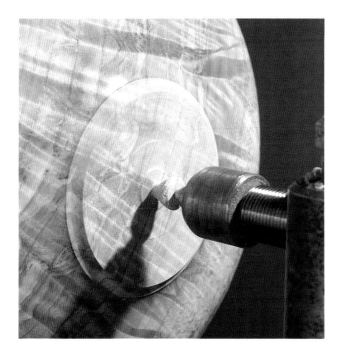

The base has been shaped and trimmed to leave a small stub in contact with the tailstock. This can be removed with a flat saw after the tailstock has been retracted.

Once the stub has been removed, the centre
of the base can be cleaned up with a gouge,
and the base may be sanded and finished.

The finished piece.

GALLERY

Wood: Cocobolo · Height: 4in (102mm)
Width: 10in (254mm) · Finish: Wax paste

Cocobolo is a beautiful timber and deserves to be shown off to its very best advantage. A closed form is a fine shape to choose in order to achieve this. In this case I followed the curve right through to the top of the blank, and finished with a delicate rim.

Wood: Burr oak and ebony · Height: 7in (178mm)
Width: 11in (279mm) · Finish: Three coats of Danish oil

*The strong patterns of the burrs in this oak draw attention
to the piece, and the shape compliments them. The ebony rim
provides a strong finish to the top of the form. This is a superb
example of the way in which burrs can enhance the decorative
impact of a piece.*

Wood: Ash · Height: 6in (152mm) · Width: 13in (330mm)
Finish: Three coats of Danish oil

*The inside wall of this closed form has a pleasing curve, which is
unusual in that it does not follow the curve of the outside. The
natural fissures were not too distracting, and I was able to
incorporate them into the design.*

Wood: Spalted beech · Height: 3in (76mm)
Width: 6in (152mm) · Finish: Melamine and paste wax

*Once again the closed form shape works hand in hand with the
wood to show off this attractive timber to its best advantage. The
strong rim makes a clear definition between the body of the work
and the inside of the form.*

Wood: Burr elm and ebony · Height: 5in (127mm)
Width: 13in (330mm) · Finish: Two coats of Danish oil

*I found the tone of this burr elm extremely attractive, and
emphasized it by turning a simple shape, adding the ebony
rim to 'contain' that simplicity.*

Wood: Spalted ash · Height: 6in (152mm)
Width: 13½in (343mm) · Finish: Three coats of Danish oil

*Here the spalted figure works in harmony with the shape,
and I decided to turn a soft inward curve at the top to guide the
eye to the interior. I also tried to keep the size of the base in a
proportional relationship to the top, thus maintaining a flowing
movement right through the piece.*

Wood: Jarrah burr · Height: 5in (127mm) · Width: 11in (279mm)
Finish: Three coats of Danish oil

The beauty, strong colour and pattern of this wood have here been combined with a shape to give it strength and a form of 'presence'. The taper of the curve has been followed through in the delicate rim. I always finish burrs with Danish oil rather than polish because polish gets into the burrs and leaves an unsightly white residue on drying.

47

The natural top turned for this chapter was made from elm, and measured 8 x 10in (203 x 254mm) as a finished piece.

CHAPTER FOUR

NATURAL TOPS

Natural tops can be turned from long grain or cross grain wood, cut from logs or burrs removed from the trunk. The piece used in the techniques section of this chapter was turned cross grained from burr elm.

These forms are challenging due to the unevenness of the rim, but they can be turned very thin using close-grained wood. Such pieces have an extreme delicacy about them reminiscent of bone china. On the other hand, those turned to a thicker and stronger form have a more rugged and rustic look to them; they remind me of old or recently excavated pottery.

The natural top form is applicable to both vase and bowl shapes, as you will see in the gallery section at the end of this chapter.

TURNING A NATURAL TOP

The original burr, cut from an elm tree.

My method of finding the 'centre' of the raw wood is to cut a disc from plywood or hardboard with a small hole in its centre. I lay this disc on the wood, positioning it as evenly as possible, and push a bradawl through the hole to secure it. Then I draw round the disc using chalk. Accuracy is difficult with this procedure, as you are working with totally rough wood, and finding the 'centre' requires a degree of guesswork and personal judgement.

Having removed the disc, I use a bandsaw or chainsaw to cut the piece as close as possible to the chalk line. A small chainsaw with a ¼in (6mm) blade is ideal for the job. This particular piece has a high point on the left; in this situation always be very careful not to snag the T-rest, or your hand, on this while turning.

The base of the blank is attached to a faceplate and mounted on the lathe. The tailstock is then brought up for safety.

Begin turning at your slowest lathe speed, to avoid excessive vibration resulting from the uneven top. The speed can be increased later as a more even cylinder emerges. Start your gouge cut at the tip of the blank and work towards the main bulk. For the initial cut, hold the gouge slightly in front of the tip, and push forward slowly until you hear a 'tick tick tick' sound, indicating that the tool is in contact with the wood and can begin cutting. Never present the gouge quickly to the wood at this stage; this can be extremely dangerous as it may be snatched from your hand. To help me see the tip and hence avoid catching it, I place a 100w spotlight behind it. Even then, caution must be exercised at all times.

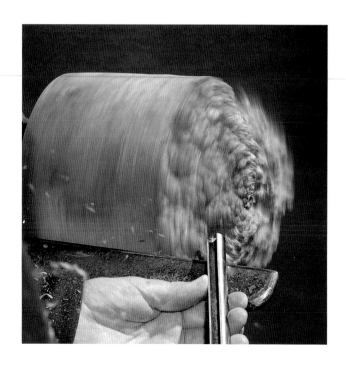

Once the outside of the bowl has been shaped, the T-rest should be repositioned securely just in front of the tip. Drill a ⅜in (10mm) diameter hole in the centre as a depth guide, and begin cutting the inside in the same way as a normal bowl.

As the hole deepens, the T-rest can be repositioned so that the right-hand end is inside the bowl itself, making cutting easier by providing closer support for the tool.

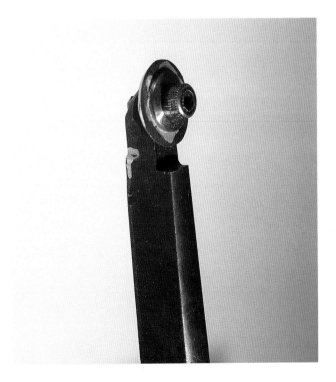

The tip of a Barton tool. This is a simple cutting and scraping tool that is ideal for cleaning up the bottom of a deep vessel. I make tool bits from industrial HSS hacksaw blades (not the bi-metal type) by cutting off the ends with the holes and grinding them to the shape I require. The remaining part of the blade makes an ideal parting tool for working on the necks of bottles.

I finished the inside using the Barton tool, but a heavy duty scraper will suffice. The final cut can be sheer, giving a finer finish.

After sanding the bowl, I used a butane torch to burn the edge for an additional decorative effect. Excess charcoal was removed with a stiff nylon brush, and the complete piece including the scorched burr, was treated with three coats of Danish oil.

To provide the necessary stability while the base of the bowl was turned down, I made a spigot to fit inside the bowl from a piece of wood measuring 1½ x 3 ½in (216 x 89mm). A hole was drilled in the end of the spigot, about ¾in (19mm) deep and just wide enough to give a snug fit over the tailstock. To prevent the spigot from marking the finished piece, I wrapped the end with jar-lid gripper material (available from hardware stores), but cloth or paper towel works just as effectively. The waste was turned away to leave a stub about ¼ to ⅜in (6 to 10mm) in diameter. This was cut away with a saw, and the base cleaned and finished.

The finished piece.

GALLERY

Wood: Burr elm · Height: 9in (229mm)
Width: 8in (203mm) · Finish: Danish oil

Here we have an open form with a dramatic ragged natural edge.
I intended this piece to be purely ornamental.

Wood: Laburnum · Height: 5½in (140mm)
Width: 7½in (191mm) · Finish: Three coats of Danish oil

*Here I made use of the fissure as part of the design. If you
compare this with the first natural top in this section it is easy to
see the slight variation that gives each piece its own individuality.*

Wood: Laburnum · Height: 6in (152mm)
Width: 7in (178mm) · Finish: Three coats of Danish oil

*This piece is a combination of a hollow form (see Chapter 6) and
a natural top. You can see that here the flow of the grain is in
perfect accord with the shape of the turning, and the pleasing
figure of the natural top links well with the edge of the bark.*

Wood: Burr maple · Height: 6in (152mm)
Width: 13in (330mm) · Finish: Two coats of Danish oil

*Here is an example of the more rugged kind of natural top piece I
mentioned in the opening of this chapter, reminiscent of recently
excavated broken pottery. I only applied two coats of Danish oil
because I wanted a sheen rather than a polished finish.*

Wood: Burr maple · Height: 6in (152mm)
Width: 13in (330mm) · Finish: Two coats of Danish oil

*A bottle shape with a natural top, turned in one go. Great care
had to be taken when cutting the uneven perimeter of the lip at
the top because during part of each revolution there was no wood
under the tool, just air. Once again only two coats of oil were
applied to achieve a sheen.*

Wood: Burr maple
Height: (from left to right) 7in (178mm), 9in (229mm), 7in (178mm)
Width: (from left to right) 6½in (165mm), 6in (152mm), 5in (127mm)
Finish: Two coats of Danish oil

Variations on a bottle form showing the types of subtly different curves which can be achieved with this kind of shape.

Wood: Laburnum · Height: 8in(203mm)
Width: 6½in(165mm) · Finish: Three coats of Danish oil

*This piece has a slightly angular shape, which allowed the top to
be wider than normal. I gave it a slight curve at the base, and
used the width to turn a generous and gently curved top. I was
fortunate to be able to retain the bark on this piece, which you can
see on the rim, and which officially makes it a natural top!*

Wood: Laburnum · Height: 6in (152mm)
Width: 5in (127mm) · Finish: Three coats of Danish oil

The lighter coloured sapwood present in this wood helped to give
a lovely movement and flow from bottom to top – this is the kind
of bonus that comes our way unexpectedly from time to time!

The vase turned for this chapter was made from laburnum, and measured 9 x 8½in (229x 216mm) as a finished piece.

CHAPTER FIVE

VASES

Vases can be turned to be purely ornamental, or designed to hold a glass container for water so that they can be used to hold fresh flowers. In turning terms, vases are tall closed forms, while those with very small openings can also be regarded as hollow forms. For an additional decorative effect they may be turned to leave a natural top including the bark or outer edge of the wood. They are pleasant shapes to turn, allowing for some really subtle curves. The main consideration is to establish a good relationship between the base and the neck when deciding on the proportion and the shape.

TURNING A LABURNUM VASE

You can cut vases from cross grain or long grain. In this case I chose long grain. The laburnum log was 10in (254mm) high and 9in (229mm) diameter.

I levelled the base of the blank with an electric hand planer, and attached a 4in (102mm) faceplate using eight 1¼in (32mm) screws. The work was then mounted on the lathe and the tailstock brought up for safety.

A ½in (13mm) gouge, ground to a fingernail shape, was used to turn the blank down to a cylinder.

Once the cylinder has been turned, the vase can be shaped. The ribbed finish on the wood is the result of pulling the gouge for a quicker cut, while the smooth surface is obtained by pushing it.

Begin shaping the top of the vase by turning from the outer rim to the centre; with long grain this is essential if you are to achieve a good finish.

Here the waste wood at the faceplate end is being removed, leaving enough body for the screws to maintain a firm hold. The bottom end of the vase can now be shaped.

Having shaped the outside of the vase, I drilled a guide hole in the centre, using a ⅜in (10mm) diameter drill bit. Masking tape wrapped around the bit acts as a simple depth mark.

Cutting the end grain from the centre to the rim using an Arizona toothpick.

The tip of an Arizona toothpick. This small, sturdy tool is a 'wood eater' and was designed by John Lea of Arizona, hence the name.

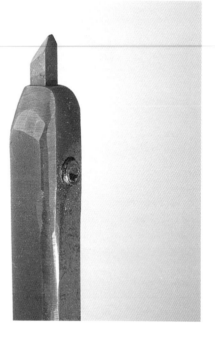

As the opening widens and deepens, a hook tool can be used to cut into the inside shoulder and turn the wall to about ½in (13mm) thick. Once the bottom of the vase has been reached, the walls can be thinned down to around ¼in (6mm).

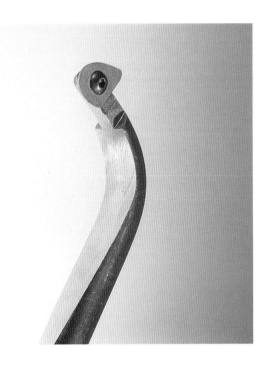

The tip of a standard 'teardrop' hook tool. This tool is generally used only for the shoulder, but with larger forms it can be used to cut depth. Depth and shoulder cutting naturally alternate as shaping progresses.

I used a cranked scraper to achieve a good finish on the inner wall, which can also be hand sanded provided you can fit your hand inside the vase!

The sanded and finished vase, ready for final turning to the base. The lighter sapwood has now become strikingly apparent.

The wide opening in the top of the vase allowed it to be mounted on expanding wood jaws fitted to a 4-jaw chuck. Then the tailstock was brought up for stability.

The waste wood was turned from the base with a small gouge at a slow lathe speed, leaving a small stub. After removing the tailstock, this was cut off, and the base sanded and finished.

The finished vase.

GALLERY

Wood: Burr elm · Height: 12½in (308mm)
Width: 7½ (191mm) · Finish: Three coats of Danish oil

*In this piece I wanted to retain the strong contrast between the
two tones which was present in the original piece of wood. I
brought the top in slightly to keep the flow of the curve and left a
very small rimmed base to balance the striking top.*

Wood: Ash · Height: 14in (356mm)
Width: 9in (229mm) · Finish: Three coats of Danish oil

*A pottery vase inspired me to experiment with a slight change of
angle to the curve of the shoulder, and this vase was the result.
The ash came from a figured burr, and the varying direction of
the grain required a great deal of patient cutting to achieve the
finished result.*

Wood: Grass tree root (*Xanthorrhoeacaea*)
Height: 14½in (369mm) · Width: 10in (254mm)
Finish: Three coats of Danish oil

Grass tree roots grow naturally in Australia, and are imported to the UK in large numbers, making them easy to obtain. They often suggest shapes themselves as this one did, the vase being turned from a large root, with the base lifted with a slight curve and the lip at the top to add interest. These roots darken considerably after turning due to oxidization on exposure to sunlight.

Wood: Cedar · Height: 8½in (216mm)
Width: 6½in (165mm) · Finish: Single coat of Danish oil

*I treated this vase with a compound of vinegar and iron filings,
which creates a chemical reaction on certain timbers, particularly
cedar, oak, walnut and elm, and turns them very dark. A single
coat of Danish oil then provided it with an added sheen.*

Wood: Figured ash burr · Height: 12½in (318mm)
Width: 9in (229mm) · Finish: Three coats of Danish oil

*This large piece was inspired by an excavated Roman vase, which
I perceived to have the kind of presence I try to achieve in all my
work. In trying to achieve the right relationship between the rim
and the base I added a slight cove to the rim, both inside and out,
to soften the line.*

78

Wood: Grass tree root · Height: 5in (127mm)
Width: 7in (178mm) · Finish: Three coats of Danish oil

The main feature of this vase is the rim, and as a result I deliberately tapered the base down to emphasize the top. The rim does not extend out over the body, as this would have appeared out of balance.

Wood: Figured ash burr · Height: 10in (254mm)
Width: 9½in (242mm) · Finish: Three coats of Danish oil

This vase has a solid, functional look about it with strong
body lines and a firm rim. The rim has a taper which leads the
eye into the vase, and, as with all my vases and bowls, the base
has a very slight concave to ensure the vase would stand flat on
the shelf or table.

Wood: Burr elm · Height: 12in (305mm)
Width: 5in (127mm) · Finish: Three coats of Danish oil

Turning deep into a long narrow body is always a challenge.
I usually try to give a very slight taper down to the base,
and then curve it gently under, so that there is no harsh
sudden line to end the base. This vase is a good example
of this approach being applied.

The hollow form turned for this chapter was made from spalted beech and measured 3½ x 6½in (89 x 165mm) as a finished piece.

HOLLOW FORMS

In 1979 I came across an article in *Fine Woodworking* on hollow turning by David Ellsworth. I was amazed by the work illustrated, and went straight out to my workshop to try a hollow form myself.

I had no bent tools and no facility to make them myself, so I had to make do with ordinary gouges. My efforts were rewarded with a hollow form, but not a particularly good one. The tools were limiting me to a fairly large opening, and I quickly saw the huge advantages of Ellsworth's bent tools. I persevered until 1988 when the Stewart system was introduced to the UK, providing me with the bent tools I needed. These allowed me to produce hollow forms with smaller openings.

Hollow forms are very challenging and require the utmost concentration and patience when turning. Since they involve blind turning through a very small opening, it is very difficult to achieve an even wall thickness. Be prepared to do a lot of careful cutting and measuring, and be patient; mastering this complex form takes time and lots of practice.

It is always best to turn the interior of a hollow form in stages (refer to the first photograph on page 84). Having shaped the exterior, drill a hole to the depth you require. Cut the entrance hole to the required size, then work your way to about half-way down, leaving the wall approximately ½in (13mm) thick. Gradually reduce the wall thickness to between ³⁄₁₆ and ¼in (5 and 6mm). The bulk in the bottom half of the workpiece simplifies cutting to the final wall thickness by reducing flexing as the wall becomes thinner.

You can turn hollow forms long or cross grained. The piece in the following technique section was turned cross grained.

TURNING A HOLLOW FORM

Cross-section of a hollow form part-way through the hollowing process. I would stop cutting down and refine the wall thickness of the top at this stage.

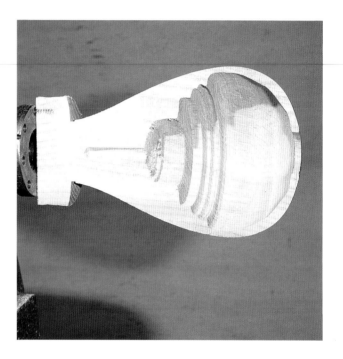

The blank was taken (with permission) from a pile of wood intended for a wood burning stove. Here, I have already made a chalk mark for the bandsaw to cut the wood into a disc measuring 6½ x 4in (165 x 102mm).

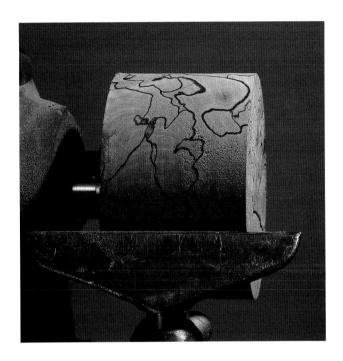

Once sawn, I planed one surface flat enough to receive a 3in (76mm) faceplate. On such a small blank the faceplate screws need not penetrate much more than ½in (13mm); four screws were sufficient for a firm hold.

I then turned the shape I had planned, using a bowl gouge. I left the rim slightly wider than required; when hollowing out the form, tools will rub the inside of the opening, and the extra wood in the rim allows any damage to be removed later on.

Once the wood had been shaped, I sheer cut it to a smooth finish with a 1½in (38mm) sheer scraper, ground to a shallow bevel. Now the exterior of the vessel could be sanded.

At this stage it is worth drilling a depth hole as a guide to prevent you from cutting too deep. I wound masking tape around the drill bit as a depth mark.

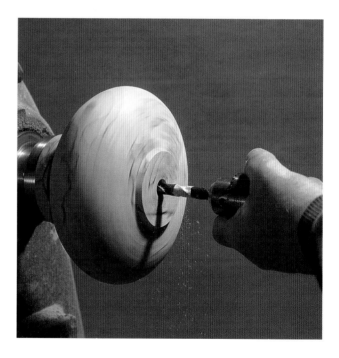

Make pencil marks to show how wide you want the entrance hole to be, and begin cutting. I used a Barton toothpick tool at this stage, widening the hole to about 2in (51mm) as I worked my way down to within ⅛in (3mm) of the bottom of the depth hole.

The tip of the Barton toothpick. This tool has a round ⁷⁄₁₆ in (11mm) mild steel shank with a hole drilled down into the rod, slightly smaller than the diagonal diameter of a ³⁄₁₆ in (5mm) drill bit and about 1in (25mm) deep. An HSS tool bit is then knocked into the end. Tools like this are excellent for hollowing out vessels, particularly if you are working through a narrow opening.

I used the hook tool from the Stewart system to hollow out the shoulder to about half-way down.

The design of the hook tool puts the cutter in line with the shank, which reduces the rotational forces on the tool that can occur when turning closed forms. As we have seen, hook tools can be fitted with a variety of interchangeable cutters; a swivel tip is shown here.

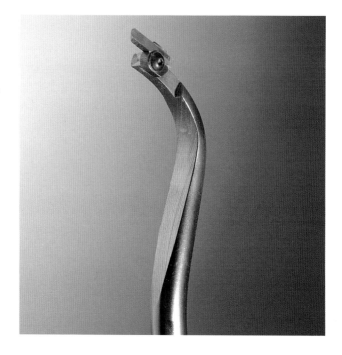

Here you can see the position of the hook tool cutting the shoulder. Ensure that only the straight part of the tool shank is on the tool rest.

You will need to stop the lathe quite frequently to measure the thickness of the walls, and empty out the shavings. A handy tool for removing the shavings, which you can use with the lathe running, is a long jam spoon fixed firmly into a handle. Hold the spoon at an angle of 45 degrees and run the lathe at normal speed; the shavings will fly out (as shown). Alternatively, a vacuum cleaner with a small nozzle, or a compressed air gun, may be used.

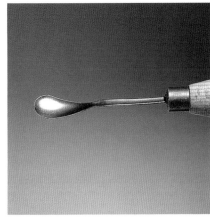

Once the piece has been hollowed out, clean up the neck and shape the rim. A miniature gouge is an ideal tool for this task.

To hold the piece while shaping the foot, cut some scrap wood into a jam-spigot with a recess for the rim.

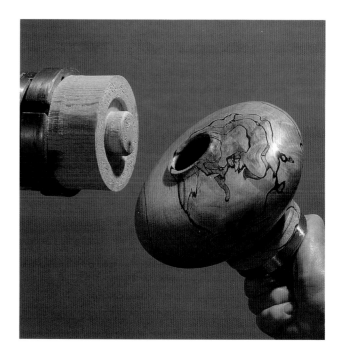

Remove the faceplate and reverse the workpiece. Use jar-lid gripper material to protect the work when it is sandwiched between the jam-spigot and the tailstock, cutting a hole in the material to fit over the spigot for good contact.

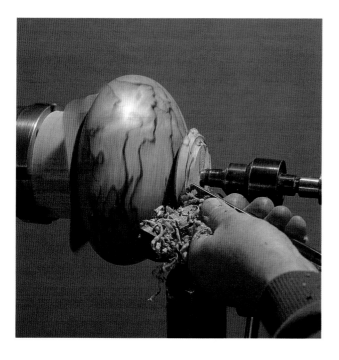

With the lathe running at a slow speed, cut away the waste wood at the base of the piece, and shape the foot.

The work is now ready to be removed from the lathe, leave a small amount of waste wood on the base.

Once off the lathe, the waste can be removed and the work sanded and finished.

GALLERY

Wood: Elm · Height: 7in (178mm) · Width: 10½in (267mm)
Finish: Three coats of Danish oil

This was an unusual piece of wood with lovely figuring which I wanted to exploit. I felt it needed a simple shape so as not to detract from the wood's beautiful appearance. I had to determine the size of the hole in relation to the size of the blank. I wanted to keep it as small as possible because, for me, this represents the ultimate challenge with these forms.

Wood: Padauk · Height: 4¼in (108mm)
Width: 7¼in (184mm) · Finish: Three coats of Danish oil

*The entrance hole to this bowl is 1in (25mm) in diameter,
and corresponded nicely with the size of the original blank from
which the bowl was turned. The top portion leading to the
entrance is indicated by a very gentle lip, making a slight
separation effect between the top and the body of the work.*

Wood: Masur birch · Height: 5in (127mm)
Width: 4½in (114mm) · Finish: Three coats of Danish oil

*I moved away from the spherical form with this piece to a slightly
more angular shape, although the base still curves gently in and
under the piece. The entrance hole is ½in (13mm) in diameter.*

Wood: Red oak · Height: 6in (152mm)
Width: 8in (203mm) · Finish: Two coats of Danish oil

This piece has a special significance to me as it was produced in David Ellsworth's workshop under his guidance. I told David I wanted to turn a sphere with as small an entrance hole as possible, and this piece with its 1in (25mm) hole was the result.

Wood: Cocobolo · Height: 4in (102mm)
Width: 6in (152mm) · Finish: Melamine and paste wax

Cocobolo is one of my favourite woods, with its wonderfully rich
colour and beautiful grain. The hollow form shape is an ideal
medium to show this wood's properties off to the full,
as you can see.

Wood: Burr maple · Height: 8in (203mm)
Width: 6½in (165mm) · Finish: One coat of Danish oil

*Here I have once again moved away from spherical shapes
and gone for a more elongated, oval shape and a gentle lip rather
than a strong rim. To retain the wood's intrinsic sheen only one
coat of oil was applied to finish.*

Wood: Padauk and ebony · Height: 4in (102mm)
Width: 7½in (191mm) · Finish: Two coats of Danish oil

*I added an ebony rim to this bowl, made from padauk, which
allowed me to make use of the full depth of the blank when
turning the bowl. The rim has a cove and has been tapered to the
entrance.*

The bottle turned for this chapter was made from American black walnut, and measured 8¾ x 6½in (223 x 165mm) as a finished piece.

BOTTLES

I really enjoy turning bottles; not only do they present a great challenge, but they are also great fun. The curves are simple and subtle.

The bodies of my bottles are hollowed out through a 1in (25mm) hole at the top, the neck being added afterwards. The main difficulty occurs when hollowing out these vessels; it is important that the wood is well secured to the lathe when cutting into end grain, as I do. As with hollow forms, shavings quickly build up inside and you will have to empty the piece frequently. I use a small suction tube which fits on to a vacuum cleaner nozzle, which helps me to do this quickly.

The reason I make my bottles from long-grained wood is to give strength to the neck, since this is of quite narrow diameter. However, you can use cross grain if you choose a contrasting, close-grain wood for the neck.

TURNING A WALNUT BOTTLE

The blank for this bottle measured 10 x 7in (254 x 178mm).

There was a natural split in the wood, (visible just above the tailstock), but the wood beneath the split was strong. I decided to turn the piece between centres so that the base could be flattened, while tapering the blank towards the base would eliminate the split.

Having removed the split, I attached the blank to a faceplate, mounted it on the lathe and turned the base down to the depth of the faceplate screws. Because I decided on a self-toned neck to the bottle, I made a thin parting line (right) to mark where the top would eventually be parted off.

Shaping of the main body has now begun. At this stage, there are still some 'flat spots' on the surface that will need removing. The problem here is that once one part of the curve has been modified, the remainder must also be altered to maintain a correct balance; this may only be a matter of careful 'fine tuning'. Always look carefully at the work at this stage to ensure that the vessel retains an even curvature. Notice also that I have formed a dovetail at the faceplate end. This provides the option of removing the piece from the faceplate and fitting it into dovetail jaws attached to a 4-jaw chuck, eliminating the need for screws and allowing me to work around the base to finish off, should this be required.

The top has now been parted off and the shape can be considered for refinement. There is still some wood left around the bottom of the bottle, which will help provide stability when the interior is hollowed out. The next stage is to drill a depth guide hole and hollow out the bottle in the same manner as a vase or hollow form (see Chapters 5 and 6).

Stop and check the wall thickness at frequent intervals. The calipers shown here are extremely useful for this task, displaying the thickness on an external gauge.

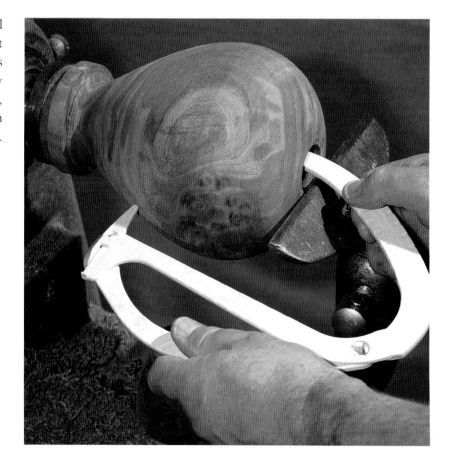

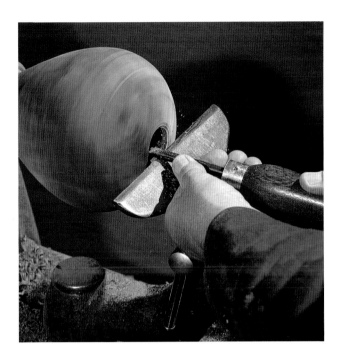

A round-section parting tool is used to clean up the inside of the opening. It is essential to hold the tool square to the workpiece. The round-section parting tool is preferable to a square-section tool, because if it touches the inside of the entrance hole, it does not mark the wall.

The top of the body must be perfectly flat where it mates with the neck. Here I am using a parting tool, held square to the workpiece, to ensure this.

Hold a rule on edge across the top of the body to check that it is perfectly flat.

Mount the wood for the neck in a 4-jaw chuck, the bottom face towards you. Then drill a ⅛in (3mm) hole completely through the centre. Use calipers to measure the width of the opening in the main body of the bottle.

Start the lathe and use the calipers to mark a fractionally larger circle on the face of the wood.

Use a parting tool to cut a shoulder approximately ⅛ to ³⁄₁₆in (3 to 5mm) wide, down to the caliper marks. Do not push the tool from thc front when making the collar, but cut from the side as shown. Pushing cuts make accuracy very hard to achieve.

Stop the lathe and offer up the body of the bottle to the shoulder of the neck. Cut the shoulder away, a fraction at a time, until it is a perfect fit.

Hollow out the bottom in a V-shape, cutting to half-way up the neck. Then remove the neck from the lathe and glue it to the body.

When the adhesive has set, the exterior shape of the bottle can be finished and sanded.

With a miniature parting tool, cut a groove around the inside of the neck. This acts as a guide when using a small gouge to hollow out the neck, preventing kickback.

Having drilled a ¼in (6mm) hole in the top of the neck, I used a small gouge to cut away the inside. Support the neck with your finger while you hollow it out, as shown here. The fine glue line where the neck is attached to the body will be dealt with next.

The glue line was removed by cutting a groove along it, effectively replacing a blemish with a decorative mark. Two further concentric grooves were also added for decoration.

Before parting off the waste, the depth of the inside of the bottle is checked with a simple depth gauge made from a steel rod and a softwood batten.

Placing the gauge along the outside of the bottle clearly shows the depth of the interior.

Here the bottom of the bottle has been shaped and I have parted off some of the base. At this stage the vessel can be given its final finish.

One method of removing the waste from the base is to make a spigot to fit inside the neck, and clean up the base using the same method as that adopted for a hollow form (see Chapter 6). Another method is shown here. A wooden collar, with a tapering rim, is mounted in dovetail jaws on a 4-jaw chuck and supports the top of the bottle while the tailstock is brought up. The collar has been cut away to show more detail; the finish of the workpiece is protected by jar-lid gripper material. This arrangement allows you to cut the waste from the bottom of the bottle, turning it down to a ¼in (6mm) diameter stub. The stub can be sawn off, and the base cleaned up.

The finished piece.

GALLERY

Wood: Burr elm · Height: 11½in (292mm)
Width: 4½in (114mm) · Finish: Three coats of Danish oil

This wood's dramatic grain led me to go for a contrast between smooth and textured surfaces, with the rim sanded smooth and the body textured with an old carbon steel scraper, ground to a V-shape, using just the tip to make the grooves. I tapered the base of the bottle very slightly to continue the effect of the tapered curve down the side.

Wood: Burr elm, cocobolo and boxwood
Height: 6in (152mm) · Width: 5½in (140mm)
Finish: Three coats of Danish oil

*A bottle made using three woods; boxwood is great to turn but is
difficult to find in good widths, so in this case it was an ideal
candidate for the spout or 'neck' of this bottle. The collar was
made from cocobolo, providing a sharper contrast to the spout and
the main body of the piece, made from burr elm.*

Wood: Beech
Height: (from left to right) 6½in (165mm),
7¼in (184mm), 5¾in (146mm)
Width: (from left to right) 4½in (114mm),
4½in (114mm), 4½in (114mm)
Finish: Spray paint

*While I would never spray or colour spectacular woods, timber
which is bland and uninteresting often benefits from this
kind of finish.*

Wood: Burr elm and boxwood · Height: 6in (152mm)
Width: 8in (203mm) · Finish: Three coats of Danish oil

*This was a beautifully figured blank, and I tried to design the
shape of the bottle so that it would show off this figuring as well
as possible. The wider than normal rim, made from boxwood,
added interest to the line of the neck.*

Wood: Maple burr · Height: 6½in (165mm)
Width: 6½in (165mm) · Finish: Single coat of Danish oil

This piece was originally turned in one, with a very narrow opening going down through the spout of the bottle. However, as sometimes happens, when I tried to make a final cut I went through the outer wall! The damage was very slight, and I decided the piece could be saved by gluing the spout on to the base. It worked well, and the join was disguised by adding the two very fine rings you can see in the photograph. Only one coat of oil was applied to this piece to give it a sheen.

Wood: Padauk and ebony · Height: 7in (178mm)
Width: 4¾in (121mm) · Finish: Three coats of Danish oil

Padauk has a strong colour but can sometimes seem rather bland.
This is overcome by turning this interesting shape and adding the
ebony rims.

119

Bibliography

Child, P. *The Craftsman Woodturner*, 2nd edn. Harper Collins, London, 1992.

Hunnex, J. *Woodturning: A Source Book of Shapes*. GMC Publications, Lewes, 1993.

Jacobson, E. *The Art of Turned Wood Bowls*. E P Dutton, NY, 1985.

James, G. T. *Woodturning Design and Practice*. John Murray, London, 1958.

Key, R. *Woodturning and Design*. B T Batsford, London, 1985.

Le Coff, A. *Lathe Turned Objects*. Wood Turning Centre, Philadelphia, 1988.

Nish, D. *Creative Woodturning*. Brigham Young University, 1975. Published in the UK by Stobart & Son, London, 1976.

Nish, D. *Artistic Woodturning*. Stobart & Son, London, 1981.

Nish, D. *Master Woodturners*. Artisan Press, South Provo, UT, 1985.

Pain, F. *The Practical Woodturner*. Bell & Hyman, London, 1957.

Pye, D. *Woodcarver and Turner*. Crafts Council, Bath, 1986.

Raffan, R. *Turned Bowl Design*. Taunton Press, CT., 1987.

Rottger, E. *Creative Woodcraft*. B T Batsford, London, 1961.

Rowley, K. *Woodturning: A Foundation Course*. GMC Publications, Lewes, 1990.

Sainsbury, J. *Guide to Woodturning Tools and Equipment*. David & Charles, London, 1989.

Taylor, V. *The Woodworker's Fact Finder*. Argus Books, Hemel Hempstead, 1988.

Thorlin, A. *Ideas for Woodturning*. Evans Brothers, London, 1977.

INDEX

A

American Association of
 Woodturners 4–5
Arizona toothpick 69,70
ash 43,46,75,78,80
Association of Woodturners
 of Great Britain 4

B

Barton tool 53–4
Barton toothpick 87
beech 26,44,116
 figured beech bowl 10–22
bent tools 83
birch, masur 95
bottles 60–1,100,101–19
 gallery 114–19
 turning 102–13
bowls 9–29
 figured beech bowl 10–22
 gallery 23–9
boxwood 29,115,117
burr ash, figured 75,78,80
burr elm 45,49–55,56,74,81,
 114,115,117
burr jarrah 47
burr maple 59,60,61,98,118
burr oak 42
burrs
 finishing 47
 natural tops 49,50–5

C

calipers 18,36,37,104,106,107
cedar 25,77
'centre', finding for burrs 50
centre finder 10
chainsaw, small 51
chucking 6
closed forms 30,31–47
 gallery 41–7
 turning 32–40
cocobolo 41,97,115
collar: for cleaning base of
 bottle 112
collar joint 35–8
cranked scraper 17,71
Crawford, Dave 4
curve 5,103

D

Danish oil 38,47,59,60
depth gauge 111
depth guide hole 13,52,69,
 83,86,104

design 5–6
dovetail 103
dovetailed spigot 12
drying out wood 31

E

ebony 42,99,118,119
Ellsworth, David 4,83,96
elm 93
 burr 45,49–55,56,62,74,81,
 114,115,117

F

figured ash burr 75,78,80
figured beech bowl 10–22
fissures 43,57,62
functional design 5

G

gloves 6
glue line 110
gouges 16,18,33,67
 miniature 21,90
 natural tops 52
grass tree root
 (*Xanthorrhoeacaea*) 76,79

H

health and safety 6
helmet, respirator 6
hollow forms 65,82,83–99
 gallery 93–9
 turning 84–92
hook tools 71,88–9
Hunnex, John
 Association of
 Woodturners of Great
 Britain 4
 Goldsmiths College 4
 influences on 3,4
 lathes 3
 one-man show at
 Ashford Gallery 4
 photography 4
 trip to USA 4–5
 The Turning Point 4

I

iron filings 77

J

jacket, work- 6
jam-spigot 90–1
jam spoon 89
James, Gerald T. 3

jarrah burr 47
jaws
 expanding wooden 20–1,
 39,72
 Mick O'Donnell jaws 11

L

laburnum 57,58,62,63
 turning a laburnum vase
 66–73
Lea, John 70

M

maple 59,60,61,98,118
masur birch 95
Mick O'Donnell jaws 11
miniature gouge 21,90
miniature parting tool 109

N

natural tops 48,49–63
 gallery 56–63
 turning 50–5
neck, bottle 106–10

O

oak 42,96
ornamental design 5

P

padauk 94,99,119
parting line 103
parting tools 36,37,105,107,
 109
polish 47
proportion 5

R

rainbow wood 24
red oak 96
red river gum 23
reference marks 10
respirator helmet 6
ribbed finish 67
rim 79
 bowls 15–17
 closed forms 31,35–8
Rottger, Ernst 3
rough-turning 12,31
round-nosed scraper 19
round-section parting tool
 105

S

safety 6

sapwood 63
scorching 54
scrapers
 cranked 17,71
 round–nosed 19
 shallow bevel to prevent
 digging in 34
 sheer 17,86
shape 5–6
shavings, removal of 89,101
sheer scraper 17,86
shoulders
 bottles 106–8
 closed forms 35–7
sisal rope 26
sonokeling 27
spalted ash 46
spalted beech 26,44
spigot 112
 dovetailed 12
 jam-spigot 90–1
 stability and natural tops 55
spray painting 116
Stewart system 83,88
swivel tip 88

T

'teardrop' hook tool 71
toothpicks
 Arizona 70
 Barton 87
Turning Point, The 4

V

vases 64,65–81
 gallery 74–81
 turning 66–73
vinegar 77

W

wall thickness 18,70,83,84,
 104
walnut 118
 turning a walnut bottle
 102–13
wenge 28
wooden jaws 20–1,39,72
work-jacket 6

X

Xanthorrhoeacaea (grass tree
 root) 76,79

Z

Zielinski, Lech 4

Titles available from Guild of Master Craftsman Publications Ltd